When the Sun Goes Down

Written by Keith Olsen
Illustrated by Geoffrey Notman

When the sun goes down and all is dark, what can you see in your yard?

Is it the flower that opens at night
or the moth that comes to drink nectar?

Is it the spider weaving the web
that catches the moth in the moonlight?

Is it the frog that wanted the moth
or the owl hunting the frog?

Is it the snail that slides down the path
or the slug that munches on plants?

Is it the insects that creep from the cracks or the mouse that hides from the cat?

When the sun goes down and all is dark, what can you see in *your* yard?